P9-CED-618

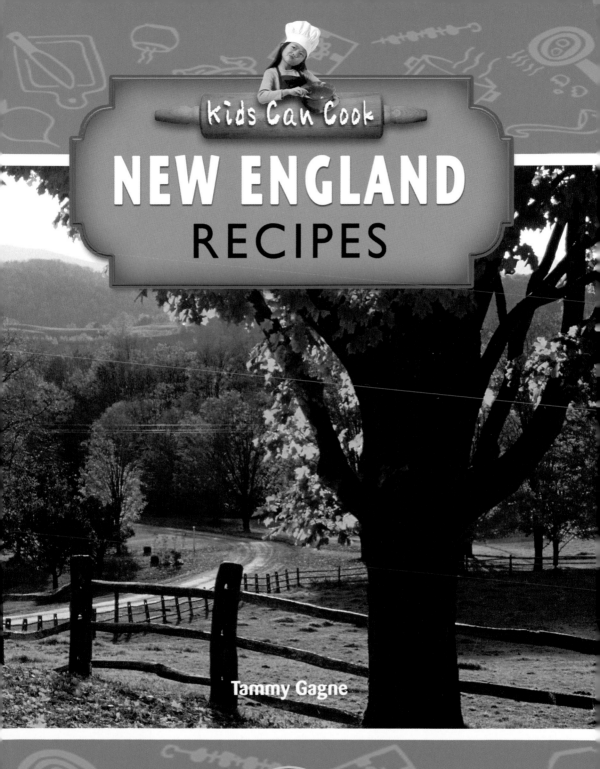

Kids Can Cook

NEW ENGLAND
RECIPES

Tammy Gagne

Mitchell Lane
PUBLISHERS

kids Can Cook

Mid-Atlantic • Midwestern
New England • Pacific Northwest
Southwestern • Western
Recipes

Copyright © 2012 by Mitchell Lane Publishers

PUBLISHER'S NOTE: The facts on which the story
in this book is based have been thoroughly
researched. Documentation of such research
can be found on page 60. While every possible
effort has been made to ensure accuracy, the
publisher will not assume liability for damages
caused by inaccuracies in the data, and
makes no warranty on the accuracy of the
information contained herein.

To my mother and grandmother, who taught
me everything I know about New England
cooking

**Library of Congress
Cataloging-in-Publication Data**
Gagne, Tammy.
 New England recipes / by Tammy Gagne.
     p. cm.
 Includes bibliographical references and index.
 ISBN 978-1-61228-067-7 (library bound)
 1. Cooking, American—New England style. I.
Title.
 TX715.2.N48G34 2012
 641.5974—dc23
                                                2011034468

eBook ISBN: 9781612281612

Printing   1   2   3   4   5   6   7   8   9

                                                        PLB

THE MENU

New England is rich with the history of the United States. One may even say it is the birthplace of the nation. Paul Revere made his historic midnight ride through Boston, Massachusetts, in 1775. Vermont became the first state to abolish slavery in 1777—nearly 84 years before the beginning of the Civil War. When the Civil War began in 1861, Rhode Island sent 24,000 soldiers (including 2,000 African American troops) to fight for the North.

The other three New England states have also played important roles in our nation's history. Noah Webster, the father of the modern dictionary, was born in West Hartford, Connecticut. Author Harriet Beecher Stowe was also born in Connecticut, but she wrote *Uncle Tom's Cabin* in Maine. Franklin Pierce, the fourteenth president of the United States, was born in Hillsborough, New Hampshire.

Just as rich as the history of this remarkable region is the food for which it is also known. New Englanders get to experience every season to the fullest. Summers are warm, perfect for picnics with lobster rolls and potato salad. Fall brings crisp air for apple picking and meandering through corn mazes. Winters are cold, allowing for activities like ice-skating and sledding—and warming up with Yankee pot roast or haddock chowder afterward. And just when you think all the snow will never melt, it does. The green returns, and New Englanders start planting the seeds to do it all again.

The fertile soil in this area grows a number of crops used throughout the United States. Maine is the largest blueberry producer in the country. Maine also has more than 400 potato farms. Vermont produces more maple syrup than any other state. It's no surprise that apple cider

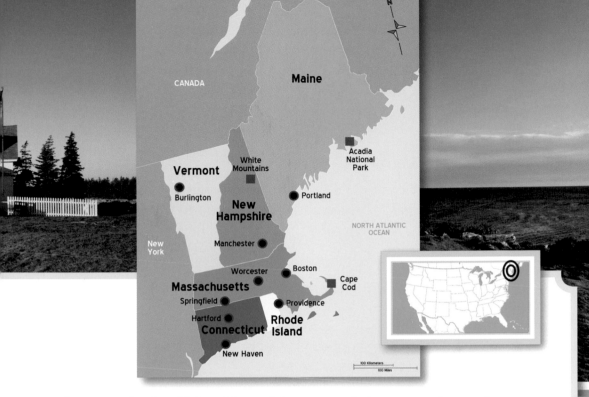

is the state drink of New Hampshire—one of the top apple producers in the nation. If you have ever had cranberry juice or dried cranberries, chances are very good that they came from Massachusetts. Connecticut is best known for its dairy farms. What does Rhode Island bring to the table? The smallest state in the continental United States produces some of the best sweet corn in the country.

Coastal New England, from northern Maine to southern Rhode Island, has some of the best seafood in the world. Generations of New Englanders have made their living on lobster boats and other fishing vessels. Other New Englanders specialize in preparing seafood for both the locals and the tourists at the many lobster pounds that dot the coastline. You will also find New England seafood on the menus of some of the finest restaurants across the country—because it is worth the cost of having it shipped.

All of these mouthwatering foods have inspired some unique recipes over the last two or three centuries. New Englanders tend to be very traditional. Many of their recipes have been handed down from generation to generation. In true New England style, however, the people from this area have always been quick to share the secrets to their culinary success.

Please work with an adult whenever a recipe calls for using a knife, a stove or oven, or boiling water.

CLAM DIP

In New England, clam dip is a party favorite. Although it adds zing to carrot or celery sticks, the traditional way to enjoy this appetizer is with some thick-cut potato chips.

Preparation time: 10 minutes
Servings: Makes about 2 cups of dip

Ingredients

6.5	ounce can of chopped clams (fresh if you can get them)
8	ounces cream cheese, softened
¾	cup sour cream
1	tablespoon minced onion
1	teaspoon minced garlic
1	tablespoon white vinegar
1	teaspoon clam juice

1. Open the can of clams and drain the juice into a container. Place the clams in a small mixing bowl.
2. Add cream cheese, sour cream, onion, and garlic. Mix at a high speed with a hand mixer for about 1 minute or until creamy. Add vinegar and clam juice and mix for about 30 more seconds.
3. Serve chilled with potato chips, crackers, or raw vegetables.

To make it healthier:
Use reduced-fat or fat-free cream cheese and sour cream.

Strawberry Salad

Strawberry picking is a fun New England pastime for both adults and children. Every June, local farms invite customers to pick their own native berries. Roadside stands stocked with countless quarts of these sweet treats also abound. Strawberries are grown in all 50 U.S. states, but there is something extra special about the ones grown in New England. It might be the slightly tart taste, or perhaps it is the fact that the growing season is so short. By July most of these berries are gone. This salad offers a healthy and tasty way to enjoy this favorite New England fruit.

Preparation Time: 15 minutes
Serves: 4

Ingredients

Salad:

6	cups of your favorite greens—for example, Romaine lettuce or spinach (or both)
8	ounces sliced Gouda cheese
1½	cups sliced strawberries
½	cup toasted, ground pecans (You can buy them pretoasted and ground)

Dressing:

¼	cup seedless strawberry jam
¾	cup extra virgin olive oil
¾	cup strawberry vinegar (or substitute red wine vinegar)

1. Wash and chop the greens, then divide them into four equal portions and arrange on salad plates.
2. Arrange cheese and strawberries on top of the lettuce on each plate. To make the salad look especially fancy, alternate the cheese wedges with the berries. Sprinkle with pecans.
3. Mix the dressing ingredients and pour over each salad just before serving.

For salads, use fresh strawberries, never frozen.

BEEF STEW

Beef stew is best served on a cold winter evening. Many New Englanders decide to make a beef stew when snow is in the forecast. Smelling this dish as it simmers in the slow cooker all day makes it taste even better at suppertime, especially if you've just come inside from sledding or shoveling.

Preparation Time: 15 minutes
Cooking Time: 8 hours
Serves: 6 to 8

Ingredients

2	small yellow onions
1	pound stew beef
4–6	white potatoes
4	large carrots
1	can green beans
1	cup beef broth
1	can cream of mushroom soup (condensed)

1. Slice onions into large chunks and place them in the bottom of a 5-quart slow cooker.
2. Place beef on top of the onions in an even layer.
3. Peel and cube the potatoes. Peel and slice the carrots. Add them and the green beans to the slow cooker.
4. In a small bowl, mix beef broth with the can of soup and pour over the other ingredients.
5. Cook on low-heat setting for about 8 hours.

To make it healthier:
Use low-sodium beef broth, low-fat cream of mushroom soup, and fresh or frozen green beans.

Haddock Chowder

There is a difference between fish chowder and haddock chowder. People who live in New England know that using the right fish makes all the difference when it comes to taste. For a less expensive version, buy chowder mix instead of haddock. Although it may consist of various types of white fish, it isn't unusual for chowder mix to be made up entirely of haddock pieces.

Preparation Time: 35 minutes
Cooking Time: 35 minutes
Serves: 6 to 8

Ingredients

4	medium white potatoes
1	tablespoon butter
2	yellow onions
1–1½	pounds of fresh haddock filets
2	cups whole milk

1. Place a large pot of water on the stove on high heat. While you are waiting for the water to come to a boil, peel and chop the potatoes. Using a large spoon to prevent splashing, carefully place them in the pot of boiling water. Reduce heat to medium and cook until potatoes are tender, about 15 minutes.
2. Peel and chop onions and sauté in butter in large frying pan. Stir periodically. Cook just until the onions are translucent.
3. When potatoes are done cooking, drain them and return them to the pot. Add onions.
4. Inspect the fish carefully, removing any bones that you find. Cut the filets into small chunks. Add to pot.
5. Simmer until fish is thoroughly cooked and chowder is fully heated, about 20 minutes.

To make it healthier:
Use a tablespoon of olive oil instead of butter, and low-fat milk instead of whole.

New England is famous for its many types of chowder, which New Englanders pronounce CHOW-dah. To make corn chowder, follow the same directions for making haddock chowder, but replace the haddock with 1 diced green pepper, 1 can whole yellow corn, 1 can cream-style corn, and 4 slices cooked bacon. When you add the milk, also add 2 cups of chicken broth.

English Muffin Pizza

As its name implies, the English muffin was invented by a Brit. Samuel Bath Thomas created the first English muffin in 1894, but he lived in New York, not England, at the time. Since then this dense bread has become a popular alternative for toast—and more. Nearly everyone in New England has had English muffin pizza at least once, more likely once in the past month or two. This petite pizza is enormously popular, largely because it is both easy to make and delicious.

Preparation Time: 10 minutes
Cooking Time: 15 minutes
Serves: 6 to 8

Ingredients

- 4 English muffins
- 1 small jar pizza sauce (or 1 cup spaghetti sauce with a pinch of oregano)
- 1 8-ounce bag shredded mozzarella cheese
- 2 ounces pepperoni, sliced
- 1 green bell pepper

1. Preheat oven to 350°F.
2. Using a fork, split each English muffin in half and place the halves face-up on baking sheet.
3. Spread each half with a tablespoon of pizza sauce.
4. Top with cheese, pepperoni, and green pepper—or whatever toppings you like on regular pizza.
5. Bake for about 10 to 15 minutes, or until cheese is fully melted.

To make it healthier:
Use whole-grain English muffins.

Variation: To make Peanut Butter and Jelly Pizza, instead of sauce and toppings, spread a tablespoon of peanut butter on each English muffin half and top with grape jelly. Pop them in the oven until the jelly starts to melt.

Fish and Chips

Originally a British meal, fish and chips has become mighty popular in New England. The chips are actually french fries, but somehow *fish and fries* just doesn't sound the same.

Preparation Time: 10 minutes
Cooking Time: 10 to 15 minutes
Serves: 4

Ingredients

1	cup flour
1	tablespoon cornstarch
½	teaspoon celery salt
¾	cup water
1¼	cups cooking oil (with ¼ cup reserved)
1½	pounds fresh cod filets
3–4	medium russet or white potatoes
	tartar sauce (optional)

For fish
1. Mix flour, cornstarch, and celery salt in a small bowl. Add water and stir until smooth.
2. Pour 1 cup of oil into a small frying pan. Place on stove at medium-high heat.
3. Inspect the fish carefully, removing any bones that you find. Cut the filets into serving-size pieces.
4. Dredge filets in batter mix and place in hot oil. Cook for 3 to 5 minutes on each side, gently turning with a pair of kitchen tongs.
5. Fry one piece at a time. When each piece finishes cooking, place it on a plate covered with paper towels. The towels will remove excess oil.

For chips

1. Preheat oven to 400°F. Peel the potatoes and slice them into long chunky strips. Place them in a small bowl.
2. Pour ¼ cup cooking oil over the potatoes and toss with a fork to coat the pieces evenly.
3. Arrange in a single layer on a baking sheet and bake for about 30 minutes, or until the fries start to brown just a bit.

The old-fashioned way to make the chips is by deep-frying them in hot oil. Working with large amounts of hot oil can be dangerous, though. Too much fried food is also unhealthy. Like people in the rest of the country, many New Englanders have realized that traditional meals can be made healthier by baking some foods instead of frying them.

Italian Sandwich

The Italian sandwich is unique to Maine. Whenever people move away from Maine, the first thing they do when they visit is buy an Italian, because they can't find these sandwiches anywhere else in the country. The Italian is indeed a ham and cheese sandwich, but it has to have these specific veggies and olive oil. Add anything, take anything away, or even toast it, and it just wouldn't be authentic. It's a Maine thing, and Maniacs (as we call ourselves) are very passionate about this sandwich.

Preparation Time: 10 minutes
Serves: 4

Ingredients

4   sub-style sandwich rolls
¼   pound deli ham
¼   pound American cheese
½   yellow onion
1   large sour pickle
1   large tomato
½   green bell pepper
¼   cup black olives
     olive oil
     salt and pepper (optional)

> Most New England sandwich shops buy their rolls from bakeries—you can, too.

1. Slice each roll from the top, about halfway through.
2. Place the ham and cheese on the bread.
3. Chop the onion and slice the pickle, tomatoes, green pepper, and black olives.
4. Divide the vegetables evenly among the sandwiches.
5. Drizzle with olive oil and sprinkle with salt and pepper, if desired.
6. Serve with potato chips.

Lobster Roll

I was born in Maine and have lived here all my life. This may mean I am a bit biased when it comes to this next recipe, but I'll say it anyway: Maine has the best lobster in the whole world. Fortunately, many Maine companies readily ship lobsters all over the United States. Even if you are on the other side of the country, you can still enjoy an authentic Maine lobster roll.

Since the cost of fresh lobster varies so much (even within New England), you can buy this ingredient in larger amounts when prices are at their lowest and freeze it until you are ready to make your lobster rolls.

Preparation Time: 10 minutes
Serves: 4

Ingredients

4	bulkie rolls (also known as kaiser rolls)
1	pound cooked lobster meat
1	tablespoon mayonnaise
¼	teaspoon chopped celery

1. Carefully slice each roll into two halves.
2. In a small bowl, mix the lobster meat, mayonnaise, and chopped celery.
3. Divide the lobster mixture evenly among the four rolls.

Replace the lobster in this recipe with 12 ounces of crabmeat, and you'll have delicious crabmeat salad—the New England version of tuna salad.

Salmon Casserole

Salmon casserole is a flavorful variation of tuna casserole. Even made with this fancier fish, this is a plain meal—that's just plain good. *Wicked good,* as a true New Englander would say. Atlantic salmon was once an abundant food source in both the ocean and the rivers running to the Atlantic coast. However, problems such as pollution and overfishing have caused Atlantic salmon populations to drop significantly. Unless you live in Maine, where Atlantic salmon is the most plentiful, you may need to substitute Pacific salmon in the recipe.

Preparation Time: 25 minutes
Cooking Time: 40 minutes
Serves: About 8

Ingredients

3	tablespoons butter
2	yellow onions
3	stalks celery
1	red bell pepper
1	orange bell pepper
1	yellow bell pepper
1	12-ounce package of egg noodles
1	large can red salmon
2	cups milk
2	tablespoons flour
½	teaspoon dry mustard
½	cup bread crumbs

1. Place a large pot of water on the stove on high heat. While you are waiting for the water to come to a boil, chop the onions. Place the onions and 1 tablespoon of butter in a large frying pan at a low-medium heat, stirring occasionally.

2. Once the water boils, place egg noodles in the pot. Cook until noodles are tender, about 10 minutes.
3. While the noodles are cooking, slice the celery and peppers. Add them to the frying pan with the onions. Keep stirring periodically.
4. Drain the egg noodles and set aside in a colander.
5. Turn on the oven to 375°F. Place flour in small bowl and add about ½ cup milk. Stir until the flour dissolves. Add the remaining milk and the dry mustard to the bowl and stir.
6. Open and drain the salmon. Place it in another small bowl, and use a fork to remove any skin or bones. Break the salmon into bite-size pieces with the side of the fork. Add it to the pan.
7. Slowly, pour the milk mixture over the salmon and vegetables.
8. Turn the heat under the frying pan up to medium, and cook until the mixture thickens, about 5 to 10 minutes.
9. Transfer the egg noodles and the salmon mixture to a greased casserole dish, stirring just enough to mix them.
10. Place the remaining butter and breadcrumbs in a small bowl and blend together with a pastry cutter.
11. Sprinkle the breadcrumb mixture over the casserole.
12. Bake for 20 minutes.

Spaghetti with Meat Sauce

Spaghetti sauce—from New England? Yes, this Italian dish is indeed a northeastern favorite. New Englanders don't make their spaghetti sauce with meatballs, though. They make it with meat sauce. This popular variation originated in Canada and came to northern New England with French-Canadian immigrants.

Preparation Time: 20 minutes
Cooking Time: 20 minutes
Serves: About 6

Ingredients

- 2 large cans stewed tomatoes
- 2 large cans tomato sauce
- 2 small cans tomato paste
- 2 tablespoons sugar
- Dash of oregano
- 1 tablespoon minced garlic
- 1 pound lean ground beef
- 1 package spaghetti

To make it healthier:
Use ground chicken or turkey instead of beef. You can also use whole-grain pasta instead of regular. Low-sodium tomatoes are also a smart choice.

1. Place tomatoes, tomato sauce, and tomato paste in a large saucepan. Add sugar and oregano and stir. Place on stove over low heat. Stir occasionally.
2. Place ground beef in a frying pan on stove over medium heat. Use a spoon to break up meat.
3. Keep stirring the meat to make sure it cooks evenly. Once it has browned, drain the fat, then add garlic and stir. Continue to cook for several more minutes.
4. Place a large pot of water on the stove on high heat. While you are waiting for the water to come to a boil, keep stirring the sauce and the ground beef.

5. When the water boils, add the spaghetti and cook until tender, about 7 minutes or according to package directions. Drain.
6. Carefully add ground beef to sauce mixture and stir. Let it simmer for about 20 minutes.
7. Place spaghetti on plates, topping with meat sauce.

Turkey Pot Pie

Making turkey pot pie is a great way to use your Thanksgiving leftovers. Although this traditional New England dish looks complicated, it is actually fairly easy. True, it takes a little time, but it is well worth the wait.

Preparation Time: 30 minutes
Cooking Time: 25 minutes
Serves: 4 to 6

Ingredients

Crust
2¼	cups flour
¾	teaspoon salt
⅔	cup shortening
8–10	tablespoons cold water

1. Place dry ingredients in a small bowl. Add shortening and mix with a pastry cutter. The results should be small crumbs.
2. Add the water, one tablespoon at a time. Mix after you add each tablespoon.
3. Using your hands, mold into two equal dough balls. Place them one at a time on a floured pastry board.
4. Using a floured rolling pin, roll each ball into a 12-inch circle. Flouring your rolling pin will prevent it from sticking to your crust.

Filling
½	pound cooked turkey
2	large or 4 small white potatoes
	Large bag mixed frozen vegetables (peas, carrots, green beans, and corn)
1	can turkey gravy

1. Preheat oven to 425°F.
2. Place bottom pie crust in pie plate and bake until golden brown, about 10 minutes.
3. Place a large pot of water on the stove on high heat.
4. While you are waiting for the water to come to a boil, peel and slice the potatoes into small cubes. Carefully place into pot. Cook about 15 minutes. Drain.
5. Cook the mixed vegetables according to the directions on the package.
6. Cut turkey into bite-sized pieces. In a medium bowl, mix turkey, potatoes, vegetables, and gravy.
7. Pour into baked pie shell and cover with remaining piecrust. Crimp the edges with your fingers and make slits in the top, so that steam can escape. (It also makes it look pretty!)
8. Bake for 10 minutes, or until top crust is golden brown.

If the edges of the piecrust start to brown too much, place aluminum foil around them while the pie finishes baking. If you are short on time, use a premade piecrust instead of making one from scratch.

Yankee Pot Roast

Yankee pot roast is a meal New Englanders make for all kinds of occasions. You will find it on the menu at holidays, when entertaining important guests, and just because it's Thursday. It is also surprisingly easy to make.

Preparation Time: 20 minutes
Cooking Time: 10 to 12 hours
Serves: 6 to 8

Ingredients

2	tablespoons cooking oil
2–2½	pound pot roast
2	yellow onions
3–4	large white potatoes
1	small bag baby carrots
2	beef bouillon cubes
2	tablespoons flour

1. Place the oil in a large frying pan and set to medium heat. Once the oil is hot, place the roast in the pan. After a minute or two, gently turn the roast over using a large pair of kitchen tongs. Browning the outside of the meat this way is called searing. Sear this side for a minute or two, as well.
2. Slice the onions into large wedges and place them in the bottom of a 5-quart slow cooker. Place the roast on top of the onions.
3. Peel and quarter the potatoes. Add to slow cooker with carrots.
4. Place bouillon in ½ cup water and pour over roast and vegetables.
5. Cook on low heat setting for 10 to 12 hours.
6. To make gravy, place flour in small bowl and add water. Stir until the flour dissolves.

7. Place about 1 cup of the juices from the slow cooker in a medium saucepan. While stirring the juices, slowly add the flour mixture. Place the pan on the stove at low-medium heat. Use a whisk to stir until gravy thickens.
8. Serve pot roast with vegetables and gravy.

Applesauce

Autumn in New England isn't just about beautiful scenery. It's also apple-picking time, which brings bushels of some of the best apples in the world. Although it can be as sweet as a dessert (or tart if you prefer), applesauce is commonly served as a side dish in this area of the country.

Preparation Time: 30 minutes
Cooking Time: 30 minutes
Serves: About 8

Ingredients

- 3 pounds of apples
- 3 cups water
- 1 cup sugar
- 1 tablespoon lemon juice
  cinnamon to taste

1. Peel, core, and chop apples into small pieces.
2. Place apples and water in large pot. Place on stove at medium heat and simmer for at least 20 minutes, stirring occasionally.
3. Continue to cook until apples break down to desired consistency. The mixture should be chunky yet saucy.
4. Add sugar and cinnamon and mix well.

Opinions differ as to which apples make the best applesauce. Some people will only make applesauce from MacIntosh apples; others insist that Cortlands are superior. Many people say the best applesauce is made from a combination of these two varieties, which are ready for picking from early September through mid-October.

Cole Slaw

In New England, cole slaw is commonly served alongside fish and other seafood dishes as well as with sandwiches. Like so many recipes from this area, this one includes apples.

Preparation Time: 15 minutes
Serves: 6 to 8

Ingredients

1   large green cabbage
4   large carrots
4   apples
1   cup non-mayonnaise salad dressing, such as Miracle Whip™ brand
4   tablespoons cooking oil
5   tablespoons apple cider vinegar

1. With a large knife, quarter and core the cabbage and slice it into long strands.
2. Using a carrot peeler, shred carrot into long, thin strands.
3. Peel and core the apples. Cut them into large chunks, small enough to fit on a fork.
4. In a separate bowl, mix salad dressing, oil, and vinegar. Pour over cabbage mixture and toss.
5. Serve cold.

MacIntosh or Paula Red apples work best for this recipe, as they are slightly tart.

Macaroni and Cheese

Macaroni and cheese has been a favorite in New England for generations. It began as a dish frequently served at church suppers. In its early days, people in southeastern Connecticut called this dish macaroni pudding.

Preparation Time: 15 minutes
Cooking Time: 30 minutes
Serves: 6 to 8

Ingredients

1	pound large macaroni
½	cup butter
2	cups half-and-half
2	large eggs, beaten
8	ounces sharp cheddar cheese, shredded
8	ounces Monterey Jack cheese, shredded
¼	cup breadcrumbs (optional)

1. Preheat oven to 350°F.
2. Place a large pot of water on the stove on high heat. When the water boils, add the macaroni. Cook until just tender, about 7 minutes. Drain and return to pot.
3. In a small saucepan, melt the butter. Take it off the heat and add the half-and-half. Mix in the eggs. Pour this over the macaroni.
4. In a large bowl, mix the cheeses, and then add them to the macaroni.
5. Transfer the mixture to a greased casserole dish. If you like a crispy top, sprinkle breadcrumbs over the rest.*
6. Bake for about 30 minutes.

* If you like your macaroni and cheese creamy, omit the breadcrumbs and stir the dish halfway through its baking time. If you bake it without stirring, the top will crisp just a bit, even without the breadcrumbs.

To make it healthier:
Use only ¼ cup of butter, low-fat cheese, and fat-free half-and-half.

Potato Salad

Potato salad is a summertime staple in New England. It is served in restaurants, on picnics—even at weddings.

Preparation Time: 30 minutes
Serves: 6 to 8

Ingredients

3	pounds red potatoes
4	eggs
¾	cup mayonnaise
¾	cup sour cream
3	tablespoons white vinegar
2	stalks celery
1	bunch of scallions

1. Place a large pot of water on the stove on high heat.
2. While you are waiting for the water to come to a boil, slice unpeeled red potatoes into cubes. Carefully add them to the boiling water. Cook about 15 minutes. Drain and run cold water over the colander, cooling the potatoes a bit. Set aside.
3. Place eggs in small saucepan. Cover with cold water. Set on stove at high heat. As soon as the water boils, place a cover on the pan and remove it from the heat. Be sure to set it on a trivet or other safe spot for a hot item.
4. Using a small bowl, combine mayonnaise, sour cream, and vinegar. Mix well and set aside.
5. Wash and slice celery and scallions. Place in large bowl. Add chopped eggs, cooled potatoes, and mayonnaise mixture. Stir well.

To make it healthier:
Use low-fat mayonnaise and sour cream and only half the egg yolks.

Boston Baked Beans

No New England cookbook would be complete without a recipe for baked beans. This favorite is most often linked with the city of Boston, but the dish is enormously popular throughout the entire region. It is rare to find a New England town without a homemade sign advertising a baked bean supper on Saturday night.

Preparation Time: Overnight + 4 hours
Cooking Time: 5 hours
Serves: 6 to 8

Ingredients

1	pound dry navy beans
¼	pound bacon
1	yellow onion
½	cup molasses
¼	cup brown sugar
1	teaspoon dry mustard

1. Rinse the beans. Place them in a large saucepan with 8 cups cold water. Cover and set aside for 6 to 8 hours, or overnight.
2. Drain and rinse the beans. Add 8 cups of fresh cold water. Set on the stove at high heat until they boil. Reduce heat to medium and simmer, covered, for 1 to 1½ hours. Stir occasionally. Drain the beans again, reserving the liquid.
3. Place the beans in a casserole dish with bacon and onion. Add 1 cup of the reserved liquid, molasses, brown sugar, and dry mustard.
4. Bake, covered, at 300°F for 2½ hours. Stir occasionally.

You may need to add more of the reserved liquid to the beans during their baking time to keep them juicy. For a vegetarian recipe, use tofu bacon or leave this ingredient out.

Apple Cinnamon French Toast

Apple cinnamon French toast can be found on the tables of many New England inns and bed and breakfasts. This popular dish can be made with any variety of apple, but the sweeter the better. The best choices are Baldwin and Red Delicious.

Preparation Time: 10 minutes
Cooking Time: 30 minutes
Serves: 4

Ingredients

- 4 eggs
- 1 cup milk
- 1 teaspoon vanilla extract
- ½ teaspoon cinnamon
- 8 slices of thick bread
  nonstick cooking spray
- 2 teaspoons butter
- ½ cup brown sugar
- ¾ cup water
- ½ teaspoon cinnamon
- 3 apples, peeled and sliced thin

1. Preheat oven to 375°F.
2. In a medium bowl, beat eggs. Whisk in milk, vanilla extract, and cinnamon.
3. Dip bread into mixture, one piece at a time. Be sure to coat it thoroughly, but don't leave it in the liquid too long.
4. Place bread on greased baking sheets. Bake for 24 minutes, turning the slices over at the halfway point.

5. Place butter and sugar in a small saucepan. Place pan on stove at low heat. Add water, cinnamon, and apples. Continue cooking on low for about 8 minutes.
6. Top French toast with apple mixture.

French toast is best when made from slightly stale bread. If you don't have any stale bread, leave your bread out on the counter for a few hours before making it.

Apple Crisp

If pot roast is the meal that is served both on holidays and everyday occasions, apple crisp is the dessert. Nearly every New England kitchen fills with the aroma of a homemade apple crisp as soon as apple-picking time arrives. A good number of homes also serve this dessert at Thanksgiving—and yet again at Christmas. It's that good.

Preparation Time: 30 minutes
Cooking Time: 30 to 35 minutes
Serves: 6

Ingredients

3	pounds apples
2–4	tablespoons sugar
½	cup rolled oats
½	cup brown sugar
¼	cup flour
¼	teaspoon cinnamon
¼	cup butter

1. Preheat oven to 375°F.
2. Peel, core, and slice apples into small pieces. Place in buttered casserole dish. Sprinkle with sugar.
3. Place remaining dry ingredients in small bowl. Add butter and use pastry cutter to combine. The mixture should look like coarse crumbs.
4. Cover apples with oat mixture.
5. Bake for 30 to 35 minutes or until slightly browned.

Serve warm and top each piece with whipped cream or a scoop of French vanilla ice cream.

Apple Scones

Scones are another British food that has become as New England as the cup of tea they are often served with. Apple scones aren't quite a dessert, but they are certainly no ordinary biscuit, either. Sweet Fuji apples are perfect for this recipe.

Preparation Time: 15 minutes
Cooking Time: 12 to 15 minutes
Serves: 4 to 6

Ingredients

2	cups flour
2	tablespoons sugar
¼	teaspoon salt
1	teaspoon baking powder
6	tablespoons butter
¾	cup heavy cream
1	apple, peeled and diced small

1. Preheat oven to 400°F.
2. Place flour, sugar, salt, and baking powder in a medium bowl and mix together.
3. Add butter and use a pastry cutter to mix until it makes coarse crumbs.
4. Make a small well in the center. Pour cream and apple into well. Mix together.
5. Transfer the dough to a pastry board and knead lightly, about a dozen times.
6. Roll out to about ½ to ¾ inches thick.
7. Cut scones with biscuit cutter and place on greased baking sheet.
8. Bake 12 to 15 minutes.

To make your scones taste even better, beat an egg and brush it onto the scones before baking.

Banana Bread Pudding

Banana bread and bread pudding have been popular New England desserts for centuries. Banana bread goes great with tea, another New England favorite. Bread pudding originated in England as a way to make use of stale bread. Early recipes were rather simple, but recent decades have offered some delicious variations. When you use banana bread instead of regular bread, for example, you end up with a sweet spin on two traditional favorites.

Preparation Time: 2 hours, if you bake your own banana bread; 20 minutes if you don't
Cooking Time: 1 hour
Serves: 6 to 8

Ingredients

- 1   boxed banana bread mix or 6 large banana muffins
- 2   bananas
- 4   eggs
- 1   cup half-and-half
- 2   cups whole milk
- ½   cup sugar
- 1   teaspoon vanilla extract

1. Bake banana bread according to package directions. Allow to cool. (If you are short on time, use 6 large banana muffins instead of making the banana bread yourself.)
2. Preheat oven to 350°F.
3. Slice banana bread into bite-sized cubes and place it on a baking sheet. Bake for about 10 minutes.
4. While the bread is toasting, peel and cut bananas into thick slices.
5. Layer cubed banana bread in casserole dish with banana slices.
6. In a medium bowl, beat eggs. Add half-and-half, milk, sugar, and vanilla extract. Whisk together until frothy.

7. Pour egg mixture over banana bread and bananas. Let stand for several minutes.
8. Bake for one hour.

To make it healthier:
Use fat-free half-and-half and skim milk. You can also reduce the amount of sugar to ¼ cup.

Blueberry Muffins

Blueberry muffins are a common breakfast item in New England kitchens. Served warm out of the oven, they go great with just about any other breakfast food. Many New Englanders like to grill them the next morning. Simply slice, butter, and place muffins butter-side down in a small frying pan set to low heat for about 5 minutes.

Preparation Time: 10 minutes
Cooking Time: 25 minutes
Serves: makes 12 muffins

Ingredients

- 2 cups flour
- 4 teaspoons baking powder
- ½ teaspoon salt
- ½ cup sugar
- 2 eggs
- 1 cup milk
- 2 tablespoons cooking oil
- 1 cup blueberries

1. Preheat oven to 400°F.
2. Mix dry ingredients in a small bowl. Set aside.
3. Beat eggs in a separate bowl. Add milk and oil.
4. Add wet ingredients to dry ingredients. Mix well.
5. Stir in blueberries.
6. Pour into greased muffin tins, filling each one about ⅔ full.
7. Bake for 20 to 25 minutes.

Be careful not to over-stir once you add the blueberries, or the batter will turn blue.

Vermont Maple Candy

Vermont Maple Candy is one of the simplest desserts to make. It has only one ingredient! Still, it is one of the sweetest New England traditions. The secret to its unique taste is using 100 percent pure maple syrup.

In spring each year, when the temperature drops below freezing at night but climbs above freezing during the day, the sap begins to rise in maple trees. "Sugarmakers" tap the trees by sinking a spout into the trunk; they place a bucket under the spout. The sap that drips into the buckets is boiled to make maple syrup.

Vermont offers consumers four different types (or grades) of maple syrup. You will pay a bit more for the Vermont Fancy grade, but this light-colored syrup offers just the right amount of sweetness and color to make this candy.

Cooking Time: 15 minutes
Makes: 18 to 20 one-ounce maple leaves

Ingredient

2 cups Vermont Fancy maple syrup

1. Pour the syrup into a large saucepan with a candy thermometer clipped to the side. Bring the syrup to a boil, stirring occasionally.
2. Once the syrup reaches 235°F, transfer the pan to a wooden cutting board to cool for about 10 minutes. Do not move the pan or stir the syrup while it is cooling. If you do, crystals will form.
3. Once the syrup temperature drops to 175°F, beat the syrup rapidly with a wooden spoon for about 5 minutes. The syrup will become lighter in color and look creamy instead of glossy.
4. Pour the syrup into rubber candy molds. These are sold at most kitchen and craft supply stores. A maple leaf mold is perfect, but you can use whatever design you like best.

5. Once the candy has cooled, turn the molds upside down to remove the pieces. If stored in a sealed container, Vermont Maple Candy will stay fresh for up to 1 month.

If you don't have candy molds, you can use a buttered pan instead. You must score the candy with a table knife as soon as you pour it into the pan. To do this, simply drag the knife through the top section of the candy in straight lines, creating small grooves. Scoring will help you separate the candy into smaller pieces once it has cooled.

Cranberry Chocolate Chip Oatmeal Cookies

Oatmeal cookies are a traditional New England treat. Adding cranberries and chocolate chips makes them even more scrumptious. Like apples and blueberries, cranberries are one of the most commonly grown crops in New England.

Preparation Time: 15 minutes
Cooking Time: 10 minutes
Makes: About 4 dozen cookies

Ingredients

½	cup butter
⅔	cup sugar
⅔	cup firmly packed brown sugar
2	eggs
1	teaspoon vanilla extract
1½	cups flour
1	teaspoon baking soda
½	teaspoon cinnamon
3	cups uncooked rolled oats
1	cup dried cranberries
1	cup chocolate chips

1. Heat oven to 350°F.
2. In a large mixing bowl, beat butter and sugars together. Add eggs and vanilla extract. Mix thoroughly.
3. In a small bowl, mix flour, baking soda, and cinnamon. Gradually add these dry ingredients to the egg mixture as you continue to mix the dough. You may need to stop using the electric mixer and hand-mix the dough toward the end.
4. Add oats, cranberries, and chocolate chips. Mix well.
5. Drop by rounded teaspoonfuls onto ungreased baking sheets.
6. Bake for 8 to 10 minutes. Let sit on top of stove for an additional 1 to 2 minutes before transferring cookies to cooling racks.

For best results, line the baking sheets with parchment paper before mounding the dough.

Pumpkin Pie

It's hard to imagine Thanksgiving without pumpkin pie. This long-loved fall dessert was made a lot differently during the time of the Pilgrims, though. It is believed that these early settlers created this favorite when they sliced off the tops of the native pumpkins, removed the seeds, and added milk, honey, and spices. The pumpkins were then baked. Over time the recipe evolved to include a pastry crust like we use today.

For this pie, you can use the piecrust recipe from the Turkey Pot Pie. You'll only need half the recipe, though, since pumpkin pie has crust only on the bottom.

Preparation Time: 25 minutes
Cooking Time: 50 to 60 minutes
Serves: 6 to 8

Ingredients

½	pie crust from Turkey Pot Pie, page 26
1	cup sugar
1	tablespoon cornstarch
	Pinch of salt
1	teaspoon cinnamon
½	teaspoon ginger
¼	teaspoon nutmeg
1	15-ounce can of pumpkin
2	eggs, beaten
1½	tablespoons butter, melted
⅛	cup molasses
1½	cups milk
	Whipped cream (optional)

1. Preheat oven to 375°F.
2. Sift dry ingredients and set them aside.
3. Place pumpkin, eggs, butter, and molasses in a medium bowl and mix together. Add dry ingredients and stir. Pour milk into mixture a little at a time and stir until combined.
4. Line the pie pan with the piecrust and bake it for 10 minutes.
5. Pour filling into the piecrust, spreading it evenly with a spatula.
6. Bake for 40 to 50 minutes. Pie is done when a knife inserted into the center comes out clean.
7. Top with whipped cream, if desired.

To prevent the crust from browning too much, place aluminum foil around the edges of the crust while the pie finishes baking. If you are short on time, use a premade piecrust instead of making one from scratch.

Johnnycake

Johnnycake is the New England name for cornbread. Traditionally, johnnycake was made in a cast-iron skillet. Due to its rough texture and heavy weight, cast iron cookware isn't as popular today as it was several generations ago. Luckily, johnnycake can also be made in a glass baking dish or metal pie pan.

Preparation Time: 10 minutes
Cooking Time: 15 to 20 minutes
Serves: 6 to 8

Ingredients

1	cup flour
1	cup yellow cornmeal
2	tablespoons sugar
2½	teaspoons baking powder
½	teaspoon salt
2	eggs
1	cup milk

1. Preheat oven to 400°F.
2. Place dry ingredients in medium bowl. Set aside.
3. Beat eggs in a small bowl. Add milk and mix together.
4. Make a well in the center of flour mixture. Pour wet ingredients into the well. Mix until just combined.
5. Pour into a greased pan, round or square.
6. Bake for 15 to 20 minutes.

If you really love the taste of corn, you can add ½ cup of frozen corn after mixing the dry and wet ingredients together.

Strawberry Frozen Yogurt

Making ice cream is a fun summertime activity. Unfortunately, it is nearly impossible to do without an ice cream maker. This recipe for frozen yogurt can be made with just a food processor or blender. It is much healthier than traditional ice cream, too.

Preparation Time: 10 minutes
Serves: 6 to 8

Ingredients

32	ounces plain low-fat yogurt
½	teaspoon vanilla extract
½	cup sugar
1	16-ounce bag frozen strawberries

1. Mix yogurt and vanilla in a small bowl. Set aside.
2. Place sugar and strawberries in a food processor and process for about 30 seconds. Continue processing 30 seconds at a time until strawberries are completely broken down.
3. Add yogurt mixture. Process for another 30 seconds, or until completely blended.
4. Serve immediately or place in freezer in an airtight container.

Once the yogurt is frozen, you must take it out of the freezer about 20 minutes before serving. Strawberry is a classic New England dessert flavor, but you can use any frozen berry (or berry combination) you like.

Further Reading

Books

Better Homes & Gardens New Junior Cookbook. Des Moines, Iowa: Meredith Corporation, 2004.

Canfield, Jack, Mark Victor Hansen, and Chef Antonio Frontera. *Chicken Soup for the Soul—Kids in the Kitchen.* Deerfield Beach, Florida: Health Communications, Inc., 2007.

Nissenberg, Sandra K. *The Everything Kids' Cookbook.* Avon, Massachusetts: Adams Media, 2008.

Works Consulted

This book is based on the author's experiences growing up and living in New England, and on the following sources:

Better Homes & Gardens New Cook Book. Des Moines, Iowa: Meredith Books, 2010.

The Culinary Institute of America: *New England Recipes.* http://www2.ciachef.edu/newengland/recipes/index.html

Staveley, Keith. *America's Founding Food: The Story of New England Cooking.* Chapel Hill: The University of North Carolina Press, 2003.

On the Internet

History.com: Pumpkin Facts
    http://www.history.com/topics/pumpkin-facts
The Lobsterman's Page
    http://www.lobstermanspage.net/index.html
New England Apple Growers Association
    http://www.newenglandapples.org/
New England Clam and Lobster Shacks
    http://www.boston.com/travel/explorene/galleries/new_england_clam_shacks/
New England Recipes
    http://www.newenglandrecipes.org/
Old Sturbridge Village
    http://www.osv.org/
Pumpkin History & Facts
    http://www.hsgpurchasing.com/Articles/pumpkin.htm
What's Cooking America: History of Italian Sandwiches
    http://whatscookingamerica.net/History/HoagieSubmarinePoBoy.htm

Resource Guide

Bar Harbor Foods—Bar Harbor, Maine
   http://www.barharborfoods.com/clam-juice.php
The Farmer's Cow—Lebanon, Connecticut
   http://www.thefarmerscow.com/
Kenyon's Grist Mill—Usquepaugh, Rhode Island
   http://www.kenyonsgristmill.com/home.html
Maine Lobster Direct—Portland, Maine
   http://www.mainelobsterdirect.com/Catalog/lobsters.cgi/Welcome.html
New Hampshire Fruit Grower's Association—Farmington, New Hampshire
   http://www.nhfruitgrowers.org/
Ocean Spray—Lakeville-Middleboro, Massachusetts
   http://www.oceanspray.com/
Stonyfield Organic
   http://www.stonyfield.com/
Vermont Maple Syrup
   http://www.vermontmaple.org/

Vermont Maple Sugar Shack

Glossary

chowder (CHOW-der)—A thick creamy soup that usually contains vegetables and seafood.

consistency (kun-SIS-tun-see)—The degree of firmness, density, and texture of an item.

crimp (KRIMP)—To pinch and press down the edges in a decorative way.

dredge (DREDJ)—To coat food by sprinkling it or by laying it in the coating material (such as flour or breadcrumbs).

immigrant (IH-muh-grunt)—A person who comes from somewhere else to settle in a new country.

knead (NEED)—To work dough with your hands to make it smooth and stretchy.

mince (MINTS)—To cut or chop into tiny pieces.

native (NAY-tiv)—Growing naturally in a particular region.

sauté (saw-TAY)—To cook gently in a frying pan with very little butter or oil.

simmer (SIH-mer)—To cook in liquid just below the boiling point.

skillet (SKIH-lit)—A shallow pan used to fry food.

translucent (trans-LOO-sunt)—Clear, see-through.

trivet (TRIV-it)—A small metal plate that holds hot dishes to protect the surface underneath it.

whisk (WISK)—To whip to a froth, or the tool used for this purpose.

Index

About the
AUTHOR

Children's book writer Tammy Gagne grew up cooking and baking alongside her parents and grandparents in their New England kitchens. One of her favorite childhood memories is baking brownies *all by herself* for the first time under her grandmother's trusting yet watchful eye. Another is listening to her mother and grandfather debate which of them made the better haddock chowder. Today Tammy prepares these and other classic New England recipes for her own family— and hopes that future generations will remember the recipes from this book as fondly as she recalls the delicious food from her own childhood.